Hope

Hope

WOLFGANG GIEGERICH

DUSK OWL BOOKS
London, Ontario, Canada

Copyright © 2024 Wolfgang Giegerich

All rights reserved.
No part of this book may be reprinted or reproduced
in any form without permission in writing from the author.

ISBN 978-1-7388606-4-7

1kxxx

Table of Contents

Sources and Abbreviations 7

Preface 9

Hope 11

1. Biological hope 15

2. Ideological hope 23

3. Metaphysical hope 35

   1. Christian hope's structural difference
      from utopian hope. 36
   2. *Who* hopes when there is Christian hope? 42
   3. The inner nature of Christian hope. 44
   4. But why hope in the first place? 47

4. Psychological hope 55

   1. Relentless commitment to horizontality 58
   2. Metaphysical hope as a standard not to fall short of. . 59
   3. The inner uroboric structure of psychological hope. . . 60
   4. The truth in the *form* of wrong presentation. 64
   5. A valid expression of the simultaneity of
      absolute boundedness and inner infinity 66
   6. "Many are the thyrsus bearers, but few are
      the true initiates." 69

Index 75

Sources and Abbreviations

For frequently cited sources, the following abbreviations have been used:

CW: Jung, C. G. *Collected Works.* 20 vols. Ed. Herbert Read, Michael Fordham, Gerhard Adler, and William McGuire. Trans. R. F. C. Hull. Princeton: Princeton University Press, 1957-1979.
Cited by volume and, unless otherwise noted, by paragraph number.

GW: Jung, C. G., *Gesammelte Werke*, 20 vols., various editors, Olten and Freiburg im Breisgau: Walter-Verlag, 1971–1983.
Cited by volume and, unless otherwise noted, by paragraph number.

Letters: Jung, C. G. *Letters.* 2 vols. Ed. Gerhard Adler. Bollingen Series XCV: 2. Princeton: Princeton University Press, 1975.

MDR: Jung, C. G. *Memories, Dreams, Reflections.* Rev. ed., Ed. Aniela Jaffé. Trans. Richard and Clara Winston. New York: Vintage Books, 1989. Cited by page number.

Erinn.: Erinnerungen, Träume, Gedanken von C.G. Jung, ed. by Aniela Jaffé, Zürich and Stuttgart (Rascher) 1967.

CEP: Giegerich, W., *Collected English Papers*, 6 vols. New Orleans, LA 2005 ff. (Spring Journal Books), now London and New York, 2020 (Routledge).

Transl. modif.: Appearing at the end of a citation, this indicates that I modified the particular quotation from the *Collected Works* in order to bring the English translation a bit closer to the wording and spirit of Jung's original German text.

Preface

During the discussion that followed the presentation of a paper of mine at a conference of the International Society of Psychology as the Discipline of Interiority in 2024 in Berlin, I was unexpectedly asked whether I could say something about the topic of hope. It may have been that the question was something like, "Is there (still) hope?". Be that as it may, this question took me by surprise, and in this situation lacking the time for further reflection I spontaneously answered that "I do not need hope", that in each situation I try to do my best and take whatever happens in my stride, a response which luckily met with approval and satisfaction from the questioner.

Even now, months later, I do not feel the need to retract what I said at that moment. But "hope" is a much larger topic so I must admit that my artless answer, all the more so because of its brevity, does not nearly do justice to it in its whole circumference and all its complexity—and depth. So now I want to look at "hope" more thoroughly. But of course, I know that with the following reflections I could not possibly exhaust this topic.

Berlin, September 2024

Hope

The topic of hope will for many people call to mind that in one of his letters[1] Immanuel Kant included the question of hope in his three oft-cited questions that according to him express the entire interest of reason and are accordingly supposed to comprise the whole spectrum of philosophy. These questions, that express "all the interest of my reason", are: "What can I know? (metaphysics)", "What must I do? (morality)", and "What may I hope? (religion)", to which a fourth question, "What is man? (anthropology)" was supposed to follow as one that overarched the other three.

We see not only that the topic of hope had a prominent place in Kant's thinking, being viewed by him as the question that defined what religion as a whole, or the philosophy of religion, was centrally concerned with, namely, so we can add, the question of the immortality of the soul. This question was nothing new. Kant had inherited it from the long-standing metaphysical tradition. For us, living in a decidedly post-metaphysical age, the question of the immortality of the soul is certainly obsolete, more than that, even the concept of "soul" underlying this question is now obsolete. It is the idea of soul that is still *imagined*, taken literally as a kind of "entity", and thus quasi "reified".

---

1   To Carl Friedrich Stäudlin, 4 May 1793.

Nevertheless, as an essential belief and as such a deep concern of our tradition, the metaphysical question of the immortality of the soul still has for the soul ("soul" now in our modern psychological sense[2]) a historical presence in *Mnemosyne* and consequently can in psychology not simply be brushed aside, despite the admitted fact that it is not and cannot be a present reality anymore. The connection of hope with what was formerly the sphere (or better dimension) of "religion" can also by us not be totally ignored. On the other hand, we must not let Kant's (here) restricting the topic of hope to this one and ultimate aspect also limit our own concerns as modern psychologists. Hope also occurs in other contexts and in other senses.

Another noteworthy aspect of Kant's formulation of his third question is that it does not really ask about the phenomenon of hope, but about *what* we may hope, what the object of hope is. But no, this is not quite correct, all the more so since "the what", the religious concern about the immortality of our soul, is already presupposed, taken over from the teachings of the long tradition of Western metaphysics and Christian religion or theology. When we look at all four questions it becomes clear that the emphasis in all of them is on the verb that changes from question to question ("can", "must", "may", and "is") in accordance with the different philosophical fields to which each question belongs, whereas the

---

[2] "Soul" in psychology is only used as a mythological *façon de parler* to refer to the hidden objective inner logic of personal as well as cultural phenomena or developments and, in an adjectival sense, to distinguish a corresponding perspective, standpoint, or quality from ordinary, everyday-life or "ego" ones.

sentence subject, "what", remains the same in all of them. So Kant's third question is really asking: "What *may* I hope?"

Significantly, as in all of the first three questions, this is a "modal verb". This shows that what Kant is really concerned with in these three questions is the *legitimacy* in each respective case of our knowledge *claims* (therefore "can"), our moral *duties* (therefore "must") and of what we *hope for* (therefore "may", i.e., "be allowed to"). Only the fourth question is no longer concerned about any legitimacy and consequently leaves the modal verbs behind because it asks for a description of the already given and permanent inner nature or essential being of Man (therefore the simple "is").

Kant's philosophical interest in "what *may* I hope?" is outside the scope of psychology. Psychology cannot say anything about the *legitimacy* of the hope for the immortality of the (metaphysically understood) soul or other religious as well as metaphysical beliefs. This does not, however, imply that psychology could and would not have its own concern about "legitimacy", including the legitimacy of specific hopes. But this is then psychological legitimacy in terms of our new (psychologically understood) concept of soul.

With his philosophical legitimacy-concern and with his *What*-question (What may I hope?) the phenomenon of hope and hoping itself is simply taken for granted by Kant here. But it as well as the *how* of hoping deserve the attention (even if not of the philosopher committed to the "entire interest of reason", but) of the psychologist.

As psychologist I have left the height of such philosophical investigations and therefore come down to the lowlands of the *phenomenology* of hope, that is to say, to its concrete reality, its rootedness in life as well as to the cultural forms and different functions that hope can have. For psychology, the phenomenon of hope manifests as a plural. There are different types of hope (and not only concrete hopes different from each other through *what* in particular is being hoped for in each case). And so I begin my discussion with a general distinction. There are three levels or types of hope:

>biological hope,
>ideological hope, and
>"metaphysical" hope,

to which I wish to add as a fourth

>"psychological hope".

1. Biological hope

It is inevitable that when we get sick we *hope* that we will recover and that when we have to take an exam we *hope* to pass it. We naturally *hope* that we will have a healthy, safe and fulfilled life, that not only our own projects will turn out well, but also that the general future development in our country or even throughout the world will be a good one. We are neither able to hope the opposite of the possible things mentioned nor not to have these hopes at all. They are in us, even if we are not conscious of them. The fact that this type of hope is inevitable is due to its being an expression of "life" as such.

Life is in itself the absolute will to live and to stay alive even under the most adverse conditions. "Hope" is thus simply our word for the life force itself, or rather, for how the propelling drive as which life exists manifests in the conscious or unconscious feelings of humans. *Dum spiro spero*, as long as I breathe, I hope (Cicero). This means that when we hope in this sense, we hope as (human) *animals*. Hope precedes and underlies our humanness. This is also why hope does not die in hopeless situations. From François de La Rochefoucauld, I believe, comes the bon mot, "Hope is the last thing that dies in man". Even if consciousness despairs, has intellectually given up all hope, has realized that there is no imaginable rescue—nevertheless underneath this insight and feeling hope still continues, only perhaps silently, unconsciously. Hope does not disappear when mere wishes *that a person has* for success, well-being, good luck, etc. are completely frustrated or when one's life is threatened, but only when the vitality, the life force itself *in a person* is mortally wounded, as, for example, in the case of both Romeo and Juliet. Persons who learned that they suffer from an advanced stage of cancer and have in all likelihood only a few weeks to live often cling all the more violently to life. This is the effect of the power of hope.

In *Prometheus Bound* (248 ff.), Aeschylus (5th century BC) lets Prometheus explain which "misdeeds" caused Zeus to punish him so severely. One of these "misdeeds" was that he prevented mortals from foreseeing their lot of having to die. Asked what cure he found for this illness of foresight, that is, how he achieved this feat, Prometheus answered that he implanted "blind hope" in mortals. Hope is seen here as being blind because it deludes people, shielding them from the truth, making them not take seriously their mortality, the fact that life's goal is death. This negative evaluation of hope was a general view in archaic Greece.

In Hesiod (fl. around 700 BC), hope is similarly one of the *evils* in Pandora's box (*Works and Days*, 53–105). The background of this negative view concerning hope is the widespread pessimistic attitude in classical Greece about life that comes out in the oft repeated dictum[3]: "Not to

---

3   Theognis (425-8), Sophocles, *Oedipus at Colonus* (1225 ff.), the anonymous *Contest of Homer and Hesiod* (315), and later Greek and Roman authors.

1. Biological Hope

be born is absolutely the best; but when a man has seen the light of day, what is second best by far is to pass through the gates of Hades as fast as possible."

I mentioned that in Hesiod, hope was one of the evils in Pandora's box. The interesting thing is, however, that whereas all the other evils came out into the world when curious Pandora opened the "box" (actually it was a jar), only hope, as one of the evils, remained in the box. This was because the moment she realized what terrible things were escaping from in the box, Pandora quickly put the lid back on; however, she was too late for meanwhile all the other evils had already escaped.

The question arises why hope was left in the box. This is counterintuitive. Would its remaining enclosed not mean that people would precisely be safe from this evil of hope? The other evils, like illness, famine, etc. can only freely unfold their effect in the human world because Pandora had let them come out of the box. As long as they were still inside the closed vessel, mankind was still safe from them. In the motif of hope as the only one of the evils that was prevented from coming out of the box we see two things, first, that as early as in this Greek story real *thinking*, an understanding of the *dialectic* of hope as an evil, is already implicitly at work, and secondly, that an imaginal narrative is not really capable of adequately expressing this clearly conceived thought. The answer to our question is: if hope had come out of the box, people would have recognized it as an *evil*. They would therefore have tried to protect themselves from this evil just as they try to protect themselves from illnesses and all the other evils. The evil of hope can precisely only work undisturbed in humans as long as it is not openly visible as the evil that it is. In contrast to all the other evils that we fear as possible threats, hope is egosyntonic. The dialectic of the innermost nature of hope *in this early Greek understanding* is that it has the power of making us hope against hope only as long as and because it hides its true nature as an evil. So that hope can be hope, we can never *face* hope, the way we face evils like an illness. Hope works from its hiding place, we could also say: from behind our backs, which confirms my earlier statement that it is an expression of the life force itself, of the animal organism's innate will to live. It is not really we who hope. It is life itself, our nature, the animal organism in us that hopes in and through us.

This means of course that to view biological hope as an evil, the way the early Greeks did, would amount to a self-dissociation, a self-contradiction, and a misunderstanding. For we are ourselves that life force that makes us hope. Our turning against our hoping would come too late. Hope has always already overtaken us as conscious beings.

Having seen that in archaic Greece this life force that also makes us hope (and this means in the last analysis "to hope against hope") was considered to be an evil, let us confront this view with another view that is expressed in Goethe's *Faust*.

Faust, for the first time confronted with Mephistopheles, asks him,

> ... Well, who art thou, then?

1. Biological Hope

Mephistopheles:

Part of that Power,
Which always wills the Bad, and always works the Good.

Faust:

What is the meaning of this riddle?

Mephistopheles:

I am the Spirit who always Denies!
And justly so: for all things that come into being
Deserve to perish:
Therefore it were better that nothing would come into being.
Thus, everything you call Sin,
Destruction, in short Evil,
That is my proper element. (1334-1344)

While Mephistopheles' statement, "it were better that nothing would come into being" perfectly tallies with the Greek "Not to be born is absolutely the best", his designation for this stance is opposite. For the archaic Greeks, it was *hope* which was an evil because it made people wish to stay alive and save themselves from having to pass through the gates of Hades as quickly as possible. Mephistopheles, by contrast, openly professes that this *his negation of life* and existence in general *is* sin, evil, indeed, that as the very spirit of negation and denial he *is* himself the very spirit of evil.

We can contrast this negative attitude towards existence also with a statement Jung made about effects that his severe illness during the year 1944 had on him. "Something else, too, came to me from my illness. I might formulate it as an affirmation of things as they are: an unconditional "yes" to that which is, without subjective objections—acceptance of the conditions of existence as I see them and understand them, acceptance of my own nature, as I happen to be." (*MDR* 297, transl. modif.)

This Jung does not need hope. In fact, hope is completely out of the question.

The unconditional yes to life is not instigated by the life force, nor does it, as hope does, have anything to do with subjective wishes, feelings, and emotions, nor is it the result of a personal ethical decision or a reaction on his part. It is not *his* affirmation at all. It is transpersonal, an objective affirmation as a simple fact, as a being, or rather as an *objective truth* that in connection with his severe illness had happened to him of its own accord and in which he found himself as a *reality* prevailing in him. While certainly contradicting the Greek negative evaluation of hope as being an evil it nevertheless goes far beyond the topic and reality of hope. It belongs to a different, higher dimension. We will come back to Jung's statement in another context.

The only thing that still remains to be done in the present context is to point out the difference between the two senses of "evil", namely, hope as *an evil*, on the one hand, and "evil" as in the case of the qualification of the negation of existence by Mephistopheles, on the other. The first is (a) a utilitarian judgement from a human, practical point of view and (b) a judgement about a particular phenomenon as object. "Evil" here means: harmful, detrimental, bad for us. The latter, by contrast, is (a) a moral judgement from the lofty standpoint of ideal principles and (b) a judgement about

1. Biological Hope

subjective attitudes, stances, and behaviors (deeds), where it means wicked, sinful, abominable.

After this clarification I can say that the designation of hope as evil (in the first sense) may itself be considered evil (in the second sense) and as not merely representing a "pessimistic" view, provided that it implicitly involves the fundamental turn against life and existence as such and provided that we adopt the lofty moral standpoint that is expressed in Goethe's definition of evil as the spirit of negation/denial (negation *on principle*!) and concretely exemplified in the statement, "Therefore it were better that nothing would come into being".

Despite this moral condemnation, I must state that the archaic Greek negative evaluation of hope and life in general has nevertheless a logically higher status than one's simply allowing hope to prevail and theoretically taking one's being alive for granted in an affirmative spirit. In the negation of the value of life, man's humanness, his freedom, his privilege and distinction, asserts itself. Notwithstanding its problematic moral status, the negative evaluation of hope bears witness to the fact that the archaic Greeks who thought this way[4] had in fact risen not only above their own animal nature but also above the *psychological* immediacy of human life as expressed in the mythological and ritualistic mode of

---

4   And I assume that this pessimistic view of life and the denouncement of hope as evil were merely thoughts, merely theoretical. Practically, in the reality of life, those who expressed such views in all likelihood still hoped and did not themselves wish to rush through the gates of Hades.

being-in-the-world. This negation is one of several phenomena that reveal that the early Greek soul—in contrast to that of all neighboring cultures, or perhaps all cultures worldwide?—had historically *truly* advanced to the *status of reflection*.

2. Ideological hope

This type of hope is called ideological because it is a brainchild. It does not have its origin in the organism's life force. It is artificial, manmade, either cooked up by the intellect or a product of people's fancy or wishful thinking. It is mainly with this type of hope in the back of my mind that my answer at that conference to the question about hope was that "I do not need hope".

An example of this type of hope born out of people's fancy is the frequent flimsy dreaming of adolescents about their future, their becoming great movie stars, popular singers, President, famous Nobel-prize winning inventors, or the like. Here it is important to note that many (not all) of such dreams do not have their real root in the personal fancy of individuals, but actually come from outside, are induced into their own fancy by fashionable images presented in social media, in magazines and books, on television, etc. A very different form of this type of hope is when in some countries after a political election the masses march through the streets overjoyed and hailing the winner or winning party in the silly belief that now everything would become better, more just, more prosperous and less corrupt.

We do not need to dwell on this type of hope any longer. It is not worth it. Only one thing needs to be added, namely, that although the form and content of this hope is a brainchild, it nevertheless receives its energy from below, from the instinctual (or drive) basis of individuals.

Another, higher-level form of this type of hope is expressed as political or philosophical ideologies with a mission for the future. The most prominent example, because of its enormous political impact, is Marxism-Leninism, but all utopias offering a vision of a possible future ideal world situation belong to this type. The philosopher Ernst Bloch even tried, above all with his book *The Principle of Hope*, to philosophically ennoble utopian thinking and to provide nothing less than a metaphysical-ontological foundation for it. According to him, not only mankind is innately driving towards a socially, spiritually, artistically as well as technologically perfect(ed) world, but also in nature itself, in the cosmos, there is an inherent upwards development from a primordial ground to a final destination.

It is easy to see that ideological hope, above all in the form of utopian thinking, is a *secularization* and, furthermore, a *corruption* and *perversion* of Christian hope. Christian hope, far from having the goal of bettering social conditions and existence in general here on earth, and even farther away from any dreaming of a paradise on earth, was once upon a time essentially, i.e., "metaphysically", oriented vertically upwards to "Heavenly Jerusalem". Man's *deepest* and *essential* striving went away from earthly reality into the heights, to the yonder. "Store up for yourselves treasures in heaven, where neither moth nor rust doth corrupt, and where thieves do not break through nor steal" (Matthew 6:20),

2. Ideological Hope

where "treasures" refers to the highest soul values. This, the beyond, heaven, transcendence, is where Christianity used to put all its hope and where Christian existence here on earth was once upon a time anchored. Accordingly, the fact that life on earth is a life in the vale of tears was simply taken for granted as inevitable. But nowadays, utopian thinking and all ideological hope locate the highest soul goal (the equivalent of the former treasures in heaven, the former Heavenly Jerusalem) decidedly down here in this world.

This corruption was necessitated by the fundamental historical rupture that (roughly around 1800) brutally severed the traditional metaphysical world from the world of modernity. As Jung put it, "The otherworldliness, the transcendence of the Christian myth was lost ..." (*MDR* p. 328). "Our age has shifted all emphasis to thisworldly man ..."; "man has been robbed of transcendence ..." (*MDR* p. 326, transl. modif.). "The value of life now lies wholly in this world ..." (*MDR* p. 265, transl. modif.). It is as if the upright vertical axis of man's being-in-the-world in the traditional world situation had suddenly been folded down onto the horizontal axis so that the highest soul value is no longer located up there in heaven, in the transcendent beyond, but hoped to be found in the nebulous distance at some point of the future on the horizontal timeline and in empirical reality. Jung's assessment indicated by my quotations is an exact description of modern reality. Verticality, and thus metaphysics, has no chance anymore in modernity. Jung had no illusions. For him, the former situation is, or rather was, an "*outdated and never recurring* world"⁵ (MDR p. 265, my italics). By stating this he at the same time indirectly struck a blow against all false prophets who try to resurrect metaphysics or claim it to be a *philosophia perennis* and thus to be possible still today as if nothing had happened historically. (I must, however admit that there are even in Jung's work and letters certain passages in which he himself sounds like one these false prophets).

But why is utopian hope not only a corruption of Christian hope, but also a perversion? In itself, there is certainly nothing wrong with the new *horizontality-only* world situation. It is not deficient, not an aberration, a decline or whatever other negative predicate we might possibly wish to assign to it. It is psychologically perfectly legitimate. The problem comes in through the fact that utopian hope does not relentlessly abide by this exclusively horizontal world situation; in its inner logic it is, so to speak, not "horizontal" enough, i.e., not exclusively "horizontal". The very point of the most prominent and paradigmatic example of modern utopian thinking, Marxism-Leninism, was to promise a paradisiacal world in empirical reality in the future, and this hoped-for distant goal was the only reason why Marxism could become so incredibly attractive to millions of

---

5   Jung is talking here about the fate of an African medicine man and the loss of his former metaphysical role. But this is of course simply a paradigmatic example for what was also our Western fate in modernity. In speaking about the medicine man, Jung spoke, psychologically seen, at the same time about himself as well as about our general psychological situation after the revolutionary change from verticality to horizontality, regardless of whether Jung was consciously aware of it or not.

2. Ideological Hope

people and particularly to so many intellectuals; and the hope for this "promised land" was also what allowed so many intelligent and personally decent people to *condone*, against all reason, all the terrible crimes against countless individuals and the masses committed by communist leaders, above all Stalin—to condone them solely in the name of the *sacred* doctrine, and *for the higher glory*, of Marxism-Leninism.

Here, with the expressions "promised land", "sacred doctrine" and "for the higher glory" the fundamental mistake inherent in Marxism-Leninism (and, by extension, in utopian thinking in general) are already laid bare. It had secretly inflated its ordinary, thisworldly socio-political program with the absolutely illegitimate metaphysical surplus value of the highest soul good appropriate only (in the Western context) to the Christian religion. Mythologically speaking, the *numen* of salvation, that was actually the property of the Christian vertical, otherworldly hope, (or, more generally, the *numen* of the sense of *the absolute*) had tacitly been taken over from Christianity and injected into this horizontal thisworldly program. Under the modern conditions of horizontality, Marxism-Leninism unconsciously was still informed by and firmly clung to the high soul value of salvation in the Christian metaphysical sense. It did not just aim for pragmatic empirical betterment, which would have been the only permissible goals under the conditions of the world situation of horizontality). So it was not the rational content of its program itself, not this program's intrinsic merit, its logical convincingness, that held so many people spellbound, but the contraband of the *numen* or *absolute value* which, for consciousness, was unwittingly hidden in it, but avidly sensed and hailed by the soul in those individuals.

The same fundamental mistake is inherent in all utopian hope, in all projects of promising and wishing to bring salvation to this world. This type of thinking, we could say, wants to have it both ways: while living in a world condition in which the horizon of human existence is irrevocably that of horizontality, it nevertheless makes use of the higher numinous power or the value of absoluteness robbed from the vertical metaphysical orientation that is by definition utterly incompatible with it. Goals for and within a strictly empirical-factual reality are inflated with higher, indeed, absolute meaning, and these programs can get away with this fraud if only their promised goals are located far enough away in the never-never future and thus out of reach. The result is a kind of fetishization, the same kind of fetishization that is inherent in the modern idea that life has an absolute value (which is behind the abolition of the death penalty). If the horizon of human existence has become exclusively that of a horizontal world and transcendence has irrevocably become a thing of the past, then nothing has absolute value and you have lost the right to hope in the sense of ideological hope. To think that life could have a higher meaning, to think that there could be an earthly paradise represents a category mistake, a logical impossibility. An absolute in the very sphere of relativity is an absurdity.

Nietzsche admonished us: *"Bleibt der Erde treu!"*

2. Ideological Hope

("Remain faithful to the earth!"[6]). For us in our context this means more specifically: Once you live psychologically under the conditions of the logic of horizontality you have to abide by it; you must not smuggle in expectations and thought structures that belong to the wholly other logic of verticality. Life is simply (and nothing more than) the way it empirical-factually just happens to turn out. No higher quasi-metaphysical value. Just facts.

The world "value" I just used brings to mind the statement we already heard from Jung that "The value of life now lies wholly in this world ...", which is his clear acknowledgment of the fact that the time of the logic of verticality is over. Our discussion so far has, however, also alerted us to the internal ambiguity, indeed, contradiction of this sentence. Read as a *speculative sentence*, what Jung's dictum really says is precisely that since the value of life is now wholly lying in this world there is no "value of life", no "highest soul value", anymore. For, the moment that this world in its thisworldliness has become the exclusive horizon and circumference of human existence, the very idea of "higher value" has become meaningless. "Value" can now only be understood banally in the two senses still reasonable in a world of horizontality, namely that of "market value" or that of subjective value, i.e., the way everyone personally values his or her own life or whatever else. A "Picasso" may have a high objective

---

[6] Nietzsche, *Thus Spoke Zarathustra*, translated by Walter Kaufmann, New York (The Viking Press), p. 13 (Zarathustra's Prologue 3).

market value, i.e., financial value, as well as be subjectively treasured by people for its aesthetic quality. In the second case "value" would, quite in keeping with the conditions of horizontality, refer to people's empirical, psychic feelings. But what is implied by "value" in Jung's phrase "the whole value of life" is something like "the whole weight of essence and importance that life has".

Jung was forced to start out his sentence with this high sense of value appropriate to the times of metaphysics in order to become able to give expression to the opposite, to the shocking quality of the tremendous revolutionary shift *from verticality to* horizontality (which entails that life does not have any value as such anymore, that is, any intrinsic, objective value). That Jung's sentence is, implicitly, self-contradictory presents, however, merely a rhetorical problem, not a case of fetishization characteristic of utopian thinking. Still, this example may alert us to the frequent cases where we unthinkingly and unwittingly still avail ourselves of the tacit metaphysical *meaning* and *feeling* invested in certain terms or ideas that we use, meanings and feelings which we as moderns are no longer entitled to enjoy and to psychologically benefit from, not even if this happens only clandestinely (unconsciously) and implicitly.

I called utopian thinking a perversion and critically analyzed its illegitimacy. As such it is inexcusable. Before, I said in my analysis that this type of thinking wants to have it both ways; it wants or at least has to be decidedly modern, to live in the world of horizontality,

2. Ideological Hope

and at the same time it wants to have the benefit of metaphysical higher values or the hope for salvation, which are only appropriate for the pre-modern world. A clear case of an objective inflation. But now I have to add that—against my verdict "inexcusable"—we must not blame the *people* of the 19th and early 20th century for this their illegitimately inflating their long-range goals for empirical reality with higher, metaphysical or soul value. Because this duplicity, as wrong and objectively indeed inexcusable as it was, was for the people themselves completely natural. It was thus simply part of the birth pangs of any transition to a radically new mode of being-in-the-world.

This is so because although *the soul* had de facto already been thrust into or rather of its own accord advanced to this new situation of horizontality and now irrevocably had its position therein, *consciousness* quite naturally lagged behind. This is because consciousness had indeed been unwittingly *thrust* into this radically new situation. It all of a sudden found itself in it without being informed that this was a totally new situation, that the accustomed logic of life in the world had been pulled out from under it and replaced by a new one. This change could remain unnoticed because the entire dimension of the *logic* of reality is invisible, hidden, not being an entity or observable process, whereas reality itself, the visible world, remained pretty much the same, thus confirming in consciousness a belief in continuity in all essential regards despite whatever empirical changes.

Thus consciousness remained tacitly but all the more powerfully still informed by the deep soul values, feelings, and longings that belonged to the bygone world situation. These values and the associated feelings, longings, indeed psychological needs, seemed to a consciousness coming from and rooted in the in truth already obsolete world situation of verticality, to be absolutely unquestionable, simply indubitable, and thus eternally valid truths without alternative. In trying to orient itself within the new situation and to make sense of it, the conscious soul was, despite its official modernity, precisely in its rational thinking as if influenced and guided from behind by the feeling patterns stemming from its past. These deep values were a "historical hangover from the past", a *caput mortuum*, as we can say with formulations Jung once used (*CW* and *GW* 10 § 363), and the fact that they continued to rule over unwitting consciousness was a telltale sign that consciousness had psychologically simply not yet fully arrived where it psychically already was.

So consciousness had to learn the hard way and all by itself. It had to be taught by reality, by, as Jung might have put it, "collision with" the symptoms or symbols of the underlying revolutionized logic, by certain absolutely novel and disturbing phenomena that were incompatible with traditional values. This learning is not only a matter of becoming intellectually aware of the changed order of things, but also of getting inwardly accustomed and *adapted* to it. And this takes time, lots of time. Maybe several centuries.

The fact that I have in this way made allowances for ideological hope, at least as it manifested during the early period of the transition to modernity, during the

2. Ideological Hope

19th and early 20th centuries, does not mean that I excuse or play down the atrocities committed in the name of utopian schemes, such as Marxism-Leninism. In fact, I think that all attempts at *putting into action* utopias as well as all forms of "rescue the world" or "salvation" schemes are on principle evil, criminal, because they are trespasses by the arrogant and free-floating intellect upon reality and a presumption, self-overestimation: hubris. Such a thing as "the world" is a priori out of empirical man's range, simply too big a bite to chew. Such wishes, even if not acted out, are in themselves forms of *logical violence*, and so it is no surprise that in practical reality they also in fact tend to result in literal compulsion, violence, and disaster.

The intellect's job is to comprehend, to achieve insight, not to grab for reality. Utopias are only legitimate as long as they have the explicit status of idle daydreams, of harmless fantasies of wishful thinking for the mind's own self-entertainment.

One often makes excuses for crimes of environmental or political activists inspired by utopian hopes because, as one says, they are motivated by "noble" *idealistic* goals, and courts often see such a motivation as a mitigating circumstance—instead of punishing idealistically-motivated crimes all the harder because of the *logical* transgression, of the betrayal of the earth inherent in them, harder at least than, *sit venia verbo*, "decent" crimes committed out of earthy human motives like greed, jealousy, hatred, etc.

3. Metaphysical hope

Now I come to the type of hope of which utopian hope was the corruption, and thus to a form of legitimate hope. Whereas all over the world there existed for people, as regards their ultimate concern, a vertical orientation, the soul's essential upward-looking, *hope* in the metaphysical or religious sense is a central issue only in the Western world and it became this issue only through Christianity. In the world of classical antiquity, hope was not a central topic in its own right, although it was certainly discussed occasionally, as we have seen in chapter 1, as well as also specifically in texts by philosophers about the "passions" (in Greek *páthê*), i.e., the human emotions or feelings, of which it was one.

Starting with Plato (*The Republic*), who was followed by Aristotle and later by the Romans such as Cicero, antiquity developed a system of four "cardinal virtues", prudence, justice, fortitude, and temperance, to which Christianity added three further virtues, often referred to as "heavenly" or "theological virtues", to bring up the total number of cardinal virtues to seven. The three additional virtues are faith, hope, love. The first mention of them together is in Paul's letters (1Thessalonians 1:3; 5:8; 1Corinthians 13:13).

Christian hope was generally the expectation of what one does not yet see. More specifically, in the New

Testament it was at first the patient expectation that Christ will come again (parousia) at the imminent end of this world, that is, still during the lifetime of the first Christians, and that he will then establish the final universal kingdom of God, which would be the beginning of a new aeon, a new cosmos. This is clearly a "horizontal" hoping along the timeline, the expectation of a (even if absolutely extraordinary) new event here on earth in the general course of events.

But in the later books of the New Testament, the emphasis of hope shifted vertically up to heaven, to the promised City of God, to "Heavenly Jerusalem". Still later, in the history of Christian theology, hope also became, and particularly so, the believers' expectation that eternal life will be bestowed on them, which includes, and essentially consists in, eternal union with God in the afterlife, more specifically: seeing God face to face and knowing him without a mirror or parable. The (second, and above all the) third understanding of hope became the accepted concept of hope in Christianity. In the practical reality of the lives of ordinary people, the hope of personally after death going to heaven what was in the foreground.

There are four points to be made.

1. Christian hope's structural difference from utopian hope. Hope as expectation, that is, as a "looking out for" some good or rather for the greatest good, the highest soul value, in the future, such as looking out for the event of Christ's second coming into this world, seems to follow the horizontal timeline, as I indicated

3. Metaphysical Hope

above. Even the hope that is in a deeper sense obviously vertical, the hope directed towards the promised Heavenly Jerusalem as well as, in fact, the notion of the beyond itself could possibly nonetheless be seen as something located on the horizontal timeline, since from a human point of view they can only be accessed in the future, after one's death (this earthly life *followed* by eternal life). Of course, death is the empirical moment in which the horizontal timeline tips up in the vertical direction. But in the personal psychology of individual believers this tipping up might merely have its place in the semantics of their belief, whereas the syntax of their actual thinking and feeling about the afterlife keeps following the horizontal timeline.

The kingdom of God, Heavenly Jerusalem, Salvation and eternal life in Heaven can, furthermore, in simple minds possible figure as no more than a desirable world totally free of the hardships and misery in reality, in other words, as a utopia. Christian hope would in this case have been absorbed into the ego's wishful thinking (just as the vertical sense of Christian hope can easily become absorbed into the ego's thinking in terms of the horizontal timeline). This projection of the highest soul value into empirical temporality would have to be judged as superstition and could rightly be said to serve as nothing but "opium for the people".

In really existing Christianity such views and feelings may certainly occur, but they would be a radical distortion of Christian hope. As always in psychology, we have to distinguish between what *people* may make (here, in our context:) of Christianity, how they receive and construe it in their own consciousness or what it becomes when it has to show itself in the dim medium of people's thinking and feeling, on the one hand, and, on the other hand, what Christianity is *for the soul* (and this means: what it in truth *is*), on the other. In the soul sense of Christianity, all these symbols, the second coming, the universal kingdom of God, Heavenly Jerusalem, salvation in afterlife, are unambiguously separated from earthly life and from the world of empirical temporality by a fundamental disruption that functions as a logical negation (*not* a positive fact in empirical reality) and assigns to those symbols the logical status of absolute negativity.

Seen in this light, it might even be possible to rehabilitate at least some of those views and feelings that certainly appear as if they were obvious distortions smacking of superstition and illegitimate appropriations of Christian hope by and for the ego. For we could say that they merely represent this hope in the medium of the imagination (*Vorstellung*) which is bound to express everything in temporal and spatial terms. It is only the mode of representation that gives to the truth the misleading form of temporality. Even if the believer as ego should indeed fall for the empirical-temporal mode of expression and thus succumb to superstition, the soul in him nevertheless hears the true meaning through the inadequate form. Likewise, what smacks of superstition from an external observer's or interpreter's ego point of view, is for the soul nevertheless what it needs and delights in. The soul understands the imaginal presentations correctly as (earthly forms *of*) absolute

3. Metaphysical Hope

negativity, or as absolute negativity merely dressed in earthly form. The soul knows how to see (or hear) through. It receives the truth even in "the impressions of the daily life" (Jung), even in distorted ego conceptions. So what simple believers with their limited understanding naively take as literal facts may *psychologically* be right on track.

It is crucial that we do not give much weight to what the ego does or thinks and how it thinks as well as expresses itself. We must not let ourselves get blinded by the surface impression made by the wording or images used or the articulation of essential contents of faith. Here, too, with one of our most essential psychological principles we have to learn to see and practice seeing "behind the impressions of the daily life, behind the scenes the *other* picture that looms up". What counts is what the soul substance of these contents is. And it is we who, as psychologists, have the duty to take the standpoint of the soul and to view, think, and feel how *it* views, thinks, and feels, not the standpoint of *people*, and not let ourselves be led astray by what *they* think and feel.[7]

In the case of myths as well as genuine fairy tales we generally practice the not-literalizing, seeing-through mode of reading them. Mythology makes it easy for us

---

[7] This reminds me of a similar problem in a completely different area of life far removed from Christian hope, namely politics. One often hears that politicians should make, or that politicians promise to make, "policies for the people" or "to serve the people". This is a fundamental error. Politicians have the job of doing what they can for the (logically negative, invisible) country, for the whole, the common weal, not for the empirically real people.

because the mythological world as well as the world of fairy tales is "one-dimensional" (Max Lüthi) in the sense that the horizon within which all soul truths, all mysteries, all gods and demons and all spirits are comprised is in myths and fairy tales solely this visible world, this real cosmos. Even the underworld and the yonder or the shaman's journey to the spirit world or the fairy-tale protagonist's journey to the "other world" "behind the seven mountains" do not leave the circumference of this real, visible world.

Christianity, however, is characterized by a fundamental division, indeed, a literal rupture, between this world and the decidedly *otherworldly* beyond. Between this world and the other world is indispensibly one's personal literal death or this world's literal doom. The two worlds are strictly incompatible with each other; the blessedness in heaven or the kingdom of God can only *be* if this life and/or this world are irrevocably over. There is an either-or that separates them. This life on earth and the beyond, this cosmos (or this aeon) and the coming universal kingdom of God are logically pairs, the one opposite in each of these pairs of opposites *is* only as the *negation of the other*, and vice versa, just as, despite their *imaginal* trimmings and embellishments, the devil is nothing but the abstract logical negation of God, hell the negation of heaven. These are all strictly logical oppositions. This also means that Christianity, *simply qua logical stage* and stage of consciousness, is logically or syntactically always already irrevocably beyond the logical status of the mythological stage of cultural development and thus also beyond the literalization of

3. Metaphysical Hope

what the imagining mode of thinking (*Vorstellung*) presents, even in cases where the conscious mind of the individual believer should still take it literally.

Christianity has lost the innocence and naivety of the mythological mind, a statement in which "naivety" is not meant critically or derogatorily; it is a descriptive term here. Christianity comes into existence on a cultural stage of consciousness that is what it is because in it the mind has been fundamentally wounded, wounded by the intrusion of reflection. In the mythological world it was possible, for example for Odysseus, to go into the underworld and return onto this earth. There were *empirical* difficulties to be overcome on the journey from here to there, but *logically* there was nevertheless a continuity between the two regions.

However, at a later time in the Western world, a cut occurred that severed this continuity and radically separates earth from heaven, this world from the beyond. This is why Christianity is itself a religion in the logical status of reflection. The notion of sin and the corresponding need for salvation reflect this status of reflection. Christianity is a decidedly *metaphysical* religion ("metaphysical" not only in the loose sense of verticality, but also in the strict sense of being informed by the logic of the copula). Its vertical orientation, at any rate, is assured from the outset.

Other religions like Islam and Buddhism are also no longer mythological. They presuppose the disappearance of the naturalism prevailing in mythologies. They exist on the level of thought and in this sense of reflection.

Nevertheless, they are not *in themselves* and explicitly wounded by negation, are not the union of mutually *exclusive* opposites, do not exist as a rift that goes through them. In other words, they have not lost their logical innocence in the same way the Western world and Christianity have. They know of course of negation and have forms of the negative in them. Zen Buddhism, for example, is centrally concerned with the Naught, with emptiness. But this Naught is the ultimate *ontological* truth of reality. That it is the ontological truth *of* the Naught saves Zen Buddhism from being *itself* logically wounded, from the negation's coming home to Zen Buddhism itself. The negation remains only semantic, a content of the teachings of Zen as well as of the Zen experience of "Awakening". It does not become syntactic.

The fact that Christianity is that religion to which the negation has explicitly and centrally come home, a religion, in other words, for which negation is no longer the object or content of consciousness (i.e., "before" it) but inherent in its own logical form, or that it is not "substance" but *subject*, this fact is absolutely unique to it.

2. *Who* hopes when there is Christian hope? The second point to be made concerns the fact that we need to leave behind our subjectivistic belief that psychological reality and thus also such a thing as hope certainly must have its origin and true home in human beings and be their personal property. By contrast, we must really take seriously the concept of the objective soul. For, Christian hope is not primordially a psychic emotion or wishing, not a subjective feeling. And it is not

3. Metaphysical Hope

really people, individuals, who hope this hope. Christian hope is a *psychological* reality, that is, an objective soul reality in its own right, an independently prevailing soul truth or logic. It has an objective existence in reality. People can be exposed to it, they can be open for it or not, they can possibly be taken hold of and permeated by it, in which case it also becomes a personal psychic reality (the logical constitution of the believer), but only then. Christian hope existed in Western culture much like other prevailing collective ideas, convictions, and prejudices formerly existed in traditional societies, quite soberly and as a matter-of-fact.

This makes it different from both biological and ideological hope. Biological hope, where it manifests, truly comes out of the vitality and instinct of survival (in the widest sense) of each individual human being in whom it manifests. It is a purely psychic reality (in contrast to an ego concoction). Ideological hope, by contrast, has on principle its true home in the generality of the intellect, and not in people, similarly to how objective soul notions prevail in the objective generality of a culture, although it came up in the mind of individuals and may also impress or even take possession of the minds of other individuals. But it is an ego product and fundamentally abstract, much like mathematics is abstract. Despite the fact of its logically residing in generality just as utopian hope does, Christian hope does not have the intellect as its source, does not have its roots in the ego of individuals, and is also not abstract, coming, as it does, out of, and belonging to, the soul.

3. The inner nature of Christian hope. As expectation, a looking out for ..., Christian hope has a direction, an intentionality. It is the soul's vertical orientation, its extendedness from down here, from this world, up to heaven. As an orientation or stance it is not, like a personal attitude, something confined and abeyant in-itself . Rather, it is within itself active, a movement, a reaching out for ..., going upwards to heaven. At the same time this hope, where it has become *embodied* in the reality of the objective soul of a culture or in an individual, is a gift of grace that inexplicably comes from above, from God (psychologically we would say: from within itself, as *causa sui*). Hope thus moves in both directions, simultaneously upwards and downwards.

Hope is Christianity's name for Man's being fundamentally more than the human animal that he is, for his always already being beyond himself, having transcended himself, *insofar as* this being-more has become actualized, a *present reality* and self-certainty in a culture or a living person. We could also say: Hope is Christianity's name for Man's twice-born-ness[8] and at the same time for this twice-born-ness having become a present reality. Jung once said, "If we understand and feel that here in this life we already have a link with the infinite, desires and attitudes change. In the final

---

8   The word "twice-born-ness" recalls to mind a passage in which Jung speaks of "the outpouring of the Holy Spirit upon the apostles, by which they were made into sons of God ... and thus partook of the certainty that they were more than autochthonous *animalia* sprung from the earth, that as the twice-born they had their roots in the divinity itself" (*MDR* p. 333). In fact, *this certainty* is itself the inner nature of Christian *hope*.

3. Metaphysical Hope

analysis, we count for something only because of the essential we embody, and if we do not embody that, life is wasted" (*MDR* p. 325). Christian hope is this objective embodiment, in a culture or in a person, of the link to the infinite, or rather not so much a link, but of the soul's in fact extending to the infinite and coming back to itself from it. As objective embodiment, it is a being (a being-so, *ein Sein*) and simply prevails; it does not need to be explicitly conscious. But it inevitably makes itself felt of its own accord and shows itself. It makes a difference in one's whole orientation, concerning what is of real importance and what not, as Jung suggests with the cited comment.

For a paradigmatic example of how this hope, as concretely embodied *cultural* reality, outwardly expressed itself we just need to look at Gothic cathedrals. They *are* this hope visibly externalized in stone; they are this the medieval soul's reaching out and upwards, thereby affirming Christian Man's certainty of being twice-born.

As the objective soul reality of the extension from down here to the yonder (rather than a subjective, private feeling as the ego's property), Christian hope is the *successor* to such mythological motifs as the *axis mundi*, the world pillar, the world ash tree whose roots are in the underworld and whose trunk goes through earthly reality and whose treetop reaches into heaven, or also to the motif of the mythological figure of Atlas who, standing on the earth, carries the vault of heaven (both keeping heaven and earth apart *and* connecting them). What also comes to mind is the Biblical Jacob's ladder.

All these mythological motifs represent the connection of heaven and earth. Seen in the light of these mythological examples we could also say that Christian hope is the name for *coniunctio* having become real in the psyche of a person or culture.

I said that Christian hope is the successor to the mythological *axis mundi*. However, it is fundamentally different from it. As (Christian) *hope*, the former "world tree" has become *inwardized, psychologized*, and *distilled*: something spiritual and an inner certainty. The "world tree" as well as all the other equivalent mythological motifs were imagined, that is to say, they were the soul idea of the *coniunctio* of heaven and earth projected into externality, into the spatial extension of the cosmos and at the same time into the (also inevitably spatio-temporal) mental world of the imagination. The *coniunctio* thus had the logical form of a thing-like (or, as in the case of Atlas, person-like) entity. It had been substantiated. (Christian) hope, by contrast, is no longer imagined as being 'something' out there. It is the soul's ability to actively *within itself* extend from down here to up there and vice versa and to *exist* as this extending or extendedness. Again: substance has become subject. This hope *is* as actuosity.

We see that what is novel in Christianity is not the content (I mean the *essential* content in contrast to the forms, actions, and images in which this content expressed itself in different cultures and on different levels of cultural development). It is much rather the same content that was at stake in Christianity as it was in the shamanistic, sacrificing, ritualistic and mytho-

3. Metaphysical Hope

logical cultures. What is novel in Christianity over against these earlier types of "religion" is solely the new logical form in which this content appeared. It has been the historical mission of Christianity to develop a *fundamentally* new "conception" or "design" of the (always same) essential content fit for the logically higher stage that the soul had meanwhile reached or that Christianity in the course of the coming centuries was destined to help give birth to, namely, the logical stage *of* logos, of spirit, logical form, the stage of inwardness, reflection, and, let me say, "alchemical" distillation.

It is not only that in Christianity "God is spirit, and those who worship Him must worship in spirit and truth" and "neither on this mountain nor in Jerusalem" (John 4:24 and 21), in other words, not by making worship dependent on particular holy places in external reality. As far as this statement goes, it is only a *semantic* truth, an assertion or declaration. But the unique feature of Christianity is that also its very *syntax* is one "in spirit" and purely of or as spirit (even if still in the misleading garb of imaginal and narrative form[9]).

4. But why hope in the first place? Hope is one of the three Christian cardinal virtues and as such used to be of central importance for Christianity. But why is hope needed? Would not the other two Heavenly Virtues, faith and love, suffice and comprise all that is needed? Obviously not, or else hope would not have been included as a third virtue. After my discussion of the nature of hope, we can also understand why. Faith only covers the

---

9 It took 18 centuries for Christianity to come truly home to itself, *objectively* come home to itself.

doctrinal content of Christianity as it is, for example, laid down in the creed in condensed form; it is, so to speak, the *"theoretical"* virtue. Love refers to the attitudinal aspect and is thus the *ethical-practical* virtue. What is still missing, but indispensable, is the *existential* aspect. Salvation, the *coniunctio* of heaven and earth, the reconciliation of God and world, Man's twice-born-ness, must not only be a semantic content of faith (a content of consciousness to be firmly believed in).

Here we need to remember that another one of the crucial novelties of Christianity is that "the Word has become Flesh", which expresses on a much higher, "alchemically distilled" spirit-level what on the more primitive, naturalistic-mythological level would be the marriage of heaven and earth and in both cases an expression of the *coniunctio oppositorum*. The virtue of faith is not enough; the *content* of faith itself concerning this *coniunctio* must in addition become embodied in Man; it must become a reality in this world, and not merely be a belief nor, through love, a pious practice (and as such become, as it were, "acted out"). It must receive the form of being, of actuality, real existence. Man (both as individual believer *and* as Man as such, as the objective soul manifest in the spirit prevailing in a given culture) must himself in his logical make-up objectively *be* this word-become-flesh, *be* this *coniunctio*, *be* the living embodiment of it. And this is what Christian hope, the way I have interpreted it, achieves, if and where it has become real.

So far so good. This insistence on the existential aspect is certainly absolutely unique to Christianity within

3. Metaphysical Hope

the range of the various major religions. But it does, of course, share this insistence on a person's or a people's (mode of) *being*, even if on a fundamentally different (logical and psychological) cultural level, with the initiating cultures. Initiation means nothing else than oneself in fact and in truth becoming in one's own existence the simultaneity of man and (a) god, in other words, becoming the 'identity of identity and difference of Man and (a) god'. There is no initiation in Christianity and there cannot be any initiation in it any longer: As *religion*, Christianity is once and for all beyond the mythological and initiating cultures and *ipso facto* beyond initiation. But under the condition of the much higher psychological level, the level of spirit and reflection, and in a logical form adequate to this higher level,[10] Christian hope is the equivalent of what primitive initiations used to be under the conditions of a *participation mystique* with nature . Under those conditions it

---

10 One might be inclined to point to the fact that within the Christian tradition there is also mysticism that aims for the *unio mystica*, the union with God. Insofar as it refers to the attempt to arrive at a spiritual experience of this union, mysticism could be considered a path of initiation on a post-mythological, post-initiating cultural level, just as the Zen way to illumination through meditation, in order to turn to at least one of the numerous wholly other cultural traditions. But the *unio mystica* as well as Zen satori are powerful *experiences* and as such *happenings*. (This is why we should not group such a *thinker* as Meister Eckhart with the mystics in the strict sense of the word, for example with Teresa of Ávila.) Christian hope, by contrast, is completely unspectacular, unemotional, quiet; it is existential, the name for a mode of being, not experiential; it a *logical truth*'s having become real: the *word's* having become flesh, as I pointed out. We could therefore perhaps say that Christian hope as heavenly virtue is Man's simply being (actually having become) the Concept in Hegel's sense.

would not only have been incomprehensible what "the Word" in the Christian phrase "the Word has become Flesh" could possibly mean, but "Flesh" would also have been taken literally, naturalistically (just think of the importance of sacrificial killings, literal ones!).

So much on Christian hope as the existential virtue. There is, however, also a second aspect, the *intrinsic character or quality* of "hope" itself. To begin with, let me say that if Christian hope can be defined as the soul's reaching out and up for the beyond, for the infinite, and to God, then this definition, *mutatis mutandis*, applies just as much to all other religions, to mention here again only the examples of Islam and Buddhism, and it applies even to all the practices of ritualistic cultures and to ancient mythologies, which logically and temporally predate religion. They all are centrally characterized by a vertical upwards orientation, but the term or idea of "hope" nevertheless does not play any essential role in them. Why was in Christianity the word hope chosen for the actual presence in Man of the vertical orientation?

The answer seems easy if we simply come back to the historical origin of hope in Christianity, the first Christians' eschatological expectation of Christ's second coming in the near future still during their own lifetime. But as I showed, this future orientation changed into the truly vertical orientation when Christianity had a bit more come into its own and home to itself after the early Christians' literalized expectation of Christ's (positive-factual) second coming had been radically disillusioned, negated (and rightly so). Again, we could make it easy for ourselves by saying that the term hope was then

3. Metaphysical Hope

retained as a kind of historical relic. But psychologically (and theologically) the term "hope", as what it authentically *became* to mean, has a deeper justification.

The term hope implies uncertainty. It has an inextinguishable future or expectation sense, and the future is on principle unknown. But in the case of Christian hope, this future sense follows the Christian logic of "is coming, and is already now here" (John 4:23). It is not yet, and yet it is already now. And also, it is already now, but nevertheless not yet. What this means is that the logical form of the virtue of hope is not that of a positivity. The fact that the existing, embodied *coniunctio* was given the name of hope means that this existing *coniunctio* itself has the logical character of absolute negativity and is understood to exist only to be an in itself *logically negative* reality. It is a certainty, as I said earlier, but one that is in itself *not* literally certain the way positive facts are certain. As absolute negativity it is a negativity, but as this negativity it is nevertheless real, a firm, existing condition of those in whom Christian hope is. And the other way around: it is a reality in them, but as this reality it has nevertheless the status or form of logical negativity.

In other words, in Christian hope *negativity* itself has become real, embodied in persons. That Christianity has negativity in its very structure is its distinction and has its place on a radically higher post-natural spirit-level.

Furthermore, the notion of "hope" is *in itself* aware of its own opposite, the possibility or threat of disappointment, disillusionment, of being totally frustrated, negated, and thus it carries this its own negation within itself. Hope is the negation of its own negation. (This is also the case of the other Christian virtue, faith, which is the negation of its negation, doubt. Only the third Christian virtue of love, in the rare cases were it has become real, is not threatened by negation because it *embraces* even what could negate it, which is probably one reason why it is, as Paul said, the greatest of the three virtues.)

If we take to heart that the dictum "the word has become flesh" is a speculative sentence so that it at the same time means that the *flesh*, i.e., the very *form of realization*, has in its inner nature become "word", *logos*, spirit, we can answer the question of why the term "hope" had to be chosen and also why hope is considered to be a virtue. How else could the reality of negativity itself or the intrinsic negativity of a psychological reality be expressed but by a term that expresses a really existing certainty which nevertheless has nothing positive to show for itself and is totally empty-handed? No proof, no guarantee, no gratification. In this way hope gives due consideration to the logical rupture that has happened, to the mind's lost innocence, the innocence inherent in the existence in the state of *participation mystique*.

Hope is defined as a virtue. Virtue generally does not so much mean an existing trait, but the vigorous *strength* to be and behave in a laudable way. Christian hope in particular is one's in fact *being* more than the human animal that one also is, one's truly being connected with the infinite, with eternity, with the absolute, one's

3. Metaphysical Hope

having one's real anchor in heaven. Hope in this sense is one's really having logically pushed off from the normal powerful feeling of the ultimate importance of life on earth and thus one's having the strength not to give so much weight to all the evils, the violence, corruption, misery and suffering that are an ineradicable part of life in *this* world. It is the strength not to have any illusions about reality, not to be overly impressed or even be shaken by terrible events and developments, nor to take all these clearly seen terrible wrongs of this world as an objection against life on earth, and above all, not to lose one's compass.

The virtue of hope is to *contra spem sperare*, to hope against hope: to live life in full responsibility to it in this world while holding one's ground in and actively *asserting* the absolute-negative *real presence* of the infinite in oneself despite the clearly seen ineradicable *hopelessness* of the empirical world, which is the place where the other Christian virtue, love, comes in. And hope is the virtue of *forgiving* the world and oneself (as part of this world, oneself as an empirical human being) for their being hopeless.

4. Psychological hope

Metaphysical hope, as exemplified by hope in Christianity, is the highest and deepest form of hope. Although this hope, where it exists, is the *inwardized* form of the mythological *axis mundi* and thus represents the analogy to Man's firm upright stance in the cosmos, his in fact *being* in himself the *coniunctio* of heaven and earth, body and soul, animal and Spirit (*Geist*),[11] it comes rather close to psychological hope. But it is of course still *metaphysical* hope and not yet psychological hope.

This is so because as long as Christianity has not come out of its *pupation as a religion*, it is still, tacitly or explicitly, subject to the mode of the imagination (the style of "imagining things", *imagining* its own essential contents). It thus inevitably perceives these essential contents within the external vertical dimension of the cosmos, with heaven and God in the heights above and us below on earth, the literal verticality. As inwardized as it already is, qua religion it still relies on the mode of

---

11 It is interesting to see how the *coniunctio*, the link, between the opposites was always substantiated and thus externalized as an entity in long the tradition from early mythological times to Descartes (when in reality Man himself *is, has to exist as,* the bond; it is not a thing but a mode of being). What for mythology was the world tree, the *axis mundi* connecting heaven and earth, was for Descartes a body organ, the pineal gland in the brain connecting body and soul. The concept and images change, the psychological issue is always the same.

Vorstellung and on the concomitant projection into "cosmological" externality: not only is the anchor of Man's existence, the anchor of Man as realized *coniunctio* and as the word *having become* flesh, still "out there", namely in heaven, but God is also still the ground of Man, Man as the word *having become* flesh. But here one might ask: where else could Man be grounded, where else could existence be anchored?

Psychology (in the soul sense of the word), this was Jung's important insight, comes into existence only through the loss of the mythological, religious, and metaphysical mode(s) of existence. For us, the loss of mythology, religion, and metaphysics is tantamount to the loss of the imagining mode, the mode of *Vorstellung* (of course not as a psychic faculty, but only concerning the essential issues of human existence). This loss is, on the one hand, the precondition of the possibility of psychology, and, on the other hand, this precondition is fulfilled in the existing condition of the modern world in which we live, because this loss is the irrevocable fact of modernity.

As Jung described it: The stars have fallen from heaven, "heaven" itself has become the meaningless positive-factual outer space of the physicists (*CW* 9/I §§ 32 and 50). The cosmos has become the vast emptiness of the universe of the astronomers in which any idea of verticality, transcendence, or "the beyond" is not only obsolete but downright absurd. The essential upwards-looking of Man has logically become impossible. The whole cosmological scheme with its principle, God, has been pulled out from under us. Now horizontality rules.

4. Psychological Hope

It is inescapable. Jung is right: "The value of life now lies wholly in this world". "Our age has shifted all emphasis to thisworldly man". We live in "an era which has concentrated exclusively upon extension of living space and increase of rational knowledge at all costs..." (*MDR* p. 325).

Man is no longer logically wrapped in the metaphysical warmth of cosmological space, which used to guarantee that the individuals were *logically* united in a great We. This objective unity was, once upon a time, a priori provided, being a cultural property. Now, logically living in the vast emptiness of the positive-factual universe and deprived of the (all-individuals-logically-unifying) cosmological wrapping, each individual is metaphysically absolutely alone and isolated, an atomic individual and in essential regards utterly thrown back upon himself. This is the objective reality.

The fact that this is the situation in which we as moderns live is our great, fundamental problem and also in particular the, it seems unsurmountable, difficulty for any survival of hope in a sense higher than that of biological and ideological hope. How can, under the conditions of irrevocable horizontality, anything like spiritual (*geistig*) hope exist?

However, we must not forget that the very loss of heaven, God, and verticality is also the *precondition* of psychology—and thus also the only chance of a truly psychological hope. But not merely the only chance, it is also the singular opportunity for and access gate to it. Indeed, the loss is even a veritable gift of history, making possible for the objective soul (not necessarily also for the individual) a decisive increase of consciousness, of which hope's becoming psychological would be a case in point.

In view of the perhaps unsurmountable difficulty of the realization of psychological hope I will only set a few signposts or guidelines.

1. Relentless commitment to horizontality. For hope to become psychological it is necessary that we resist the temptation to look backwards and cling to the old world situation of verticality and transcendence, let alone the temptation of attempting to rescue or restore them. We must not wish to *get out* of the strictly horizontal orientation or to compensate for it, but on the contrary, get deeper into it, more relentlessly committed to it. For this is where the soul's truth is in our age, in modernity. This is why Jung emphasized one's being inexorably thrown back upon oneself in one's irrevocable *psychological* loneliness: "In an era which has concentrated exclusively upon extension of living space and increase of rational knowledge at all costs, it is a highest demand to become conscious of one's uniqueness and limitation" (*MDR* p. 325, transl. modif.). And "the highest and decisive experience of all" is "to be alone with one's self .... The patient must be alone in order to experience what it is that supports him when he [I clarify, he as ego] can no longer support himself" (*CW* 12 § 32, transl. modif.). We must radically break with the metaphysical world—which is inevitably a fake metaphysical world in our time—, which also means: we must systematically remove all remaining so tenacious traces of it from our

4. Psychological Hope

thinking and feeling.

But in the last sentence I have against my will succumbed to the language of the ego: "*We must* break with...", "*we must* remove ...". In reality, we must not do any such thing, since the break has already happened objectively, of its own accord. It lies behind us. The only thing needed is that this comes home to ourselves and gets integrated into the structure of our consciousness and accordingly changes our expectations and feelings. For this to happen, we cannot do much. It must be done to us. All we can do is to intellectually prepare consciousness for it.

2. Metaphysical hope as a standard not to fall short of. Although it must become clear to us that the time of metaphysics and of the possibility of metaphysics lies irrevocably behind us, nevertheless, psychological hope must not fall below the standard set by metaphysical hope. Jung's dictum is still valid: "The decisive question for man is: Are you related to something infinite? This is the criterion of his life" (*MDR* p. 325, transl. modif.). This is the test question, the standard and measure by which the individual is ultimately to be judged: "In the final analysis, we count for something only because of the essential we embody, and if we do not embody that, life is wasted" (*MDR* p. 325). A harsh judgement, but simply true.

And certainly, Jung is absolutely right when he says: "It is not ethical principles, however lofty, or creeds, however orthodox, that lay the foundations for the freedom and autonomy of the individual, but simply and solely the empirical awareness, the unambiguous experience of an intensely personal, reciprocal relationship between man and an extramundane authority which acts as a counterpoise to the 'world' and its 'reason'" (*CW* 10 § 509, transl. modif.).[12] Indeed, all the ethical principles and belief-systems are nothing but pious ego stances and incapable of serving as a substitute for a real and indispensable counterpoise to the "world" and its "reason".

3. The inner uroboric structure of psychological hope. *Formally, structurally*, it is easy to describe what makes hope psychological: Hope must be fully interiorized into *itself*. Then it is no longer a hoping *for* something, something to come in the future, and thus it has this something no longer as its object or goal outside of itself. It has become self-contained, self-sufficient. It has both its own fulfillment and its ground[13] in itself, and also exists as Man's ground and anchor, that anchor that metaphysical Man had in God. In other words, it has become and thus *is* itself what hope used to *hope for*, inasmuch as it is the *manifestation* of the infinite, that infinite which Jung, still in the style of metaphysical parlance, said one has to be related *to*. But one cannot

---

[12] The only thing to be criticized in this dictum is the word "experience" (*Erfahrung*). Psychology is not based on inner experiences, which are happenstance empirical events. Psychology (and thus also psychological hope) relies on the *knowledge* of the psychological truth (or psychological truths in general). Experiences can certainly be helpful, but merely as triggers, stepping stones or midwives toward such a knowledge, not more.

[13] "What supports him when he as ego can no longer support himself."

4. Psychological Hope

relate to infinity in the context of *psychological* hope. It is, provided that it in fact *is*, a person's *being*. It is, then, realized, embodied, alive in him or her or as he or she.

How can psychological hope in itself *be* what it used to hope for? Here I have to come back to the earlier insight that Christian hope had the form of certainty (even if a certainty with an inherent negativity) as well as to the idea presented in footnote 12 above that psychology relies on knowledge and not on inner experiences that contingently may happen to a person. The answer to our question must be that in psychological hope, hope must have taken on the *logical form* of conceptual knowledge. In this form it is indeed no longer expecting and wishing for anything to come in the future. Knowledge is satiated in itself. Having become a knowing, hope has come home to itself.

To understand this better we must remember that infinity is the innermost truth and essence of the *humanness* of the human *animal* or we could also say: of Man's transcendentality, and that this humanness is not given (fulfilled) by birth, is not anything natural (empirical, positive-factual), but is merely the human animal's vocation or task and has to be produced by Man himself, both culturally and by each individual biographically. The task is to make Man's transcendentality, his *determination*, real; to make the *implicit* humanness of the human animal (and especially the innermost essence of this humanness) *explicit*, to give it actual presence in this life and in this finite world, to truly embody it. Man has to give birth to himself as human.

That the ultimate truth of Man's humanness is this humanness's own inner infinity results from the fact that it is not a part of the finite world. Man's humanness does not have its origin in the finite world, but inexplicably originates *contra naturam* from within *itself*. It is *causa sui*. It is not conditioned by finite reality, not dependent on it, not affected by it. Furthermore, logically, it is absolute negativity and can never become a positive fact. And thus it is, insofar as it in fact *is*, the existence of *freedom*.

All this means that infinity is a highly sophisticated truth that for the primitive, naturalistic and childlike mind could only appear in projected form, namely projected into the external space of the cosmos or of the imagination. Historically speaking, infinity as the core of the humanness and transcendentality of the human animal was therefore, on the level of mythological/ritualistic culture, a present reality *in acted-out form*, and on the cultural level of religions a present reality *in imaginal form*, the form of *Vorstellung*, in which form it was imagined as unending spatial extension or as eternity in the sense of *sempiternitas*, unending duration.

In modernity, under the conditions of horizontality, infinity has a chance, no more than a chance, of becoming a present reality *in its true form* because it now can possibly *come home to itself*. For us, therefore, the infinite must no longer be projected and imagined. It can be inwardized into in itself. That infinity that is at stake in our context must be conceived as absolute-negative "quality", not as a limitless extension. We could perhaps use words like "depth" or "freedom" for this "quality". In

4. Psychological Hope

its truth, infinity is the name for the logical form of the movement of uroboric self-generation-and-return-into-itself, of circularity.

Christian hope, I said, was the successor to the mythological *axis mundi* and, so to speak, its inwardization into the truly Christian Man, namely as his upright vertical orientation and unshakeable stance. Psychological hope is also the whole Man's firm stance, but no longer a vertical upwards-looking, because the cosmological "above" and "beyond" no longer exist in a world that is irrevocably horizontal.

Nevertheless, the name "hope" in "psychological hope" for the explicit realization of infinity as the innermost core of Man's humanity can with some justification be retained. This is so because the "reaching out" inherent in the meaning of the term "hope" is still present in psychological hope as interiorized into *itself*, of course no longer as an expectation of something to come, but now as Man's knowing that he himself *exists* as *internal* extendedness from "empirical animal" to the absolute negativity of infinity, that he exists as inner self-transcendence, mythologically speaking, as his himself *being* the *coniunctio* of heaven and earth. While Christian hope was the completely inwardized mythological *world tree* within the cosmological scheme of divine heaven above and earth below, psychological hope is, in addition, the absolute inwardization into Man of this whole outer cosmological scheme, in which he used to be enveloped, and of its fundamental verticality.

But the "knowing" in the phrase "knowing that he

himself *exists* as *internal* extendedness" can easily be misunderstood. In everyday life as well as in science, knowledge usually refers to the intellect's or the ego's knowing *something about* something. Thus we could think that psychological hope implies our knowing something *about* our true nature as internally self-transcendent beings. But the knowing at stake in our context of psychological hope is something completely different. It is the soul's knowing in a really existing individual as *homo totus*, as the whole man. As such it is this person's *real being*, a fully embodied knowing, simply his true identity, self-feeling, and real stance in life—*living* psychological hope.

4. The truth in the *form* of wrong presentation. It was Jung's psychologistic mistake, a fundamental error, to believe that the infinite (or the relation to the infinite) could be sought and found through what he called the individuation process that would in the course of time lead to the encounter and (numinous) experience of certain dream images of "*the* self". The infinite on the level of true psychology can on principle not be sought and found and particularly not introspectively in oneself: because it is not something *in* oneself, since if it is, it is the innermost truth of this total "me", my innermost being as the whole person that I am. Either I myself *am* in my innermost core this infinity and *am* Jung's "extramundane[14] authority which acts as a counterpoise

---

14 Naturally, in the present psychological context "extramundane" is not to be understood in the literal cosmological sense where it would mean superterrestrial. It expresses only that it does not come out of the empirical world, is free of worldly interests and emotions: because it has its origin *in itself*.

4. Psychological Hope

to the 'world' and its 'reason'" *or* I am not.

Jung comes much closer to the truth when he connects the feeling for the infinite with one's being bounded to the utmost, one's knowing that "I am *only* that!" and one's being unique in his personal combination—that is, *ultimately* limited—and adds that "only then!" can the infinite become conscious (see *MDR* p. 325). He comes with these ideas closer to the truth because with them Jung's sole focus is correctly on *totum hominem*, on the individual *as a whole* and as a really existing human being, instead of being concerned with what goes on "inside" him, with images coming "from his unconscious". And secondly, by nailing Man down to his empirical uniqueness (and atomic individuality) as his confinement in his being "*only* that!", Jung relentlessly follows the modern law of horizontality and its empiricism.

Nevertheless, how Jung said what he said in the cited passages about the indispensable awareness of one's individual uniqueness and limitation is unfortunately still hampered by the language of ego feeling and experiencing as well as by the idea of one's "attaining" access to the infinite. What he described in this unfitting form of expression is in reality the insight into an objective logical truth, into the *logic* of the inseparableness that exists between the (possibly) happening event that a person's utter limitation, his being locked in himself, has fully come home to him, on the one hand, *and* this person's own innermost *real* infinity, on the other. Similarly, what Jung wants to say in his sentence, "Only consciousness of my absolute (*engsten*) confinement in the self is attached to the limitlessness of the unconscious" (*MDR* p. 325, transl. modif.), is certainly essential, but the way he articulates it is unfortunate. For, I am of course not absolutely confined in *the self*, but "in myself", in the real "me" that I am, which is my true "wholeness". By substantiating "self", Jung has abstracted from "myself as the real "me" an Other, an "it": "*the* self", and split "me" into me and this invented entity, "the self". Furthermore, the expression, "the limitlessness of the unconscious", evokes the image of an endlessly ongoing spatial extension in all directions, which is misleading.

5. A valid expression of the simultaneity of absolute boundedness and inner infinity. What is really meant when Jung speaks of the result of the full awareness of one's absolute confinement in oneself becomes—indirectly—further clarified by a passage part of which I had already occasion to quote in the first chapter about biological hope. As a reminder, this passage comes from Jung's report about a very serious illness from which he had to suffer in 1944.

> Something else, too, came to me from my illness. I might formulate it as an affirmation of things as they are: an unconditional "yes" to that which is, without subjective objections—acceptance of the conditions of existence as I see them and understand them, acceptance of my own nature, as I happen to be. ... / It was only after the illness that I understood how important it is to affirm one's own destiny. In this way we forge *an I that does not break down when incomprehensible things happen; an I that endures, that endures the truth, and that is capable of coping with the world and with fate* (*MDR* p. 297, transl. modif., my italics).

4. Psychological Hope

Here I first need to note that it is not at all *we*, as Jung suggests here, who "forge" this I. As he indicated clearly enough before, the unconditional "yes" to that which is had come to him from his illness. This illness, as a fact of real life, was what brutally forged him into his *real* "I am *only* that!" and forced him into his simple naked identity with himself, the identity with the reality and truth as which he exists. And, by *in fact* doing this, it laid bare his own innermost infinity that gave him this new psychological faith, i.e., the unconditional "yes" as that "extramundane authority which acts as a counterpoise to the 'world' and its 'reason'" and, as a result of this "yes", "an I that endures, that endures the truth, and that is capable of coping with the world and with fate"[15] (transl.

---

15   We may wonder here why late Jung, long after having become this "I that endures the truth" about the world and fate and that affirms its destiny with this unconditional "Yes!", nevertheless felt the need to consider the "problem of evil" as the great problem of our time as well as the future ("We stand face to face with the terrible question of evil, and one is not even aware of it, let alone of how to answer it" *MDR* p. 331, transl. modif.) and, furthermore, why he, quaternity-fixated, wished, like the Gnostics, to lodge the antinomy of Good and Evil in the Deity itself. From the point of view of soul, and thus for psychology, the principle of Evil, Satan, the Devil, is merely the *substantiated*, still "mythologized" and literalized presence, in the Christian scheme, of *absolute negativity*, of that negativity that would be Christianity's own inner logical character the moment it ceased to be held down in the form of religion. And, on the other hand, the God who IS *Love*, which means: has gone under into Love, been sublated into Love (so that now *this* objective Love is what once was God, and thus is the new infinite, the ultimate reality), is not the one side of the antinomy (what a banal understanding of *this* no longer harmless, but verily "terrible" Love this would be!). It is the real sublation and distillation of the antinomy as a whole:

modif.). This is the inner uprightness and unshakeableness of the inwardized former world tree—of course, this inwardized successor to the mythological world tree no longer as Christian hope grounded in the God in heaven, but as self-contained psychological hope.

It is "destiny", real reality, that counts in these regards, not the "relations between the ego and the unconscious", not any introspective experience of images from "the unconscious", not the mandala pictures painted by Jung during the years 1916–1918 that gave rise to his (problematic) theory of "the self".[16] And again, it is the whole man, the real person body and soul, and not "the ego" nor "the self", these split-off abstractions, who are confronted (*if* such a confrontation takes place) with the infinite that they themselves in truth *are*.

---

precisely what Jung actually sought but, so it seems, could not reach (because, clinging to the substantiating mode of thinking, he did not see that what Christianity was ultimately about, what psychologically Christianity's historical task and very function was, is nothing else but to bring, and to initiate the soul into, absolute negativity).

16 About those mandala pictures Jung wrote: "I saw how the self, that is, my wholeness was at work" (*Erinn.* p. 199 my translation, cf. *MDR* p. 197.). *We* see here how Jung makes out of his wholeness a separate other, an it, thus distinguishing (if not *logically* dissociating) himself from it. The problem of experiencing images of "the self" or numinous images in general is that what psychologically is essential is whether the experience (or the experienced image) transforms the logical constitution of the experiencing person as a whole, not whether the image is seen, understood, felt by him or her and, maybe, a cause for ethical action by him. All these latter possibilities, often demanded by Jung, are psychologically beside the point.

4. Psychological Hope

6. "Many are the thyrsus bearers, but few are the true initiates."[17] We have seen that Christian hope was in addition to a psychic reality in individual believers also an objective cultural reality that expressed itself even in external reality, for example, in the phenomenon of Gothic cathedrals. Psychological hope, by contrast, is only a possibility for individuals. Whether it could ever also become a cultural reality and an objective and simply prevailing truth for the generality is in the lap of the gods. If so, it could only be thought of as something in the very distant future. For the present and the near future, psychological hope is exclusively a matter of personal psychology.

Psychotherapy is, on principle, for everybody. Likewise, the idea upheld by Jungian analysts is that ideally the individuation process in Jung's sense should be gone through by every individual. But our topic, psychological hope, refers to something that on principle is possible only in a few individuals who possess the needed soul strength, inner fineness, personal honesty, and above all the inner depth of soul. It is something like a gift of grace, and so it seems to be achievable only for special people. Most people have simply no need for it, being satisfied to live on the level of the modern form of *panem*

---

17 A Greek saying, maybe of Orphic origin and quoted by Plato (*Phaedo* 69c), makes the difference between perfunctory participants in mystery rites and those for whom those rites result in a transformation of the logic of their mode of being-in-the-world, to which Plato adds that "true initiates" should for him be understood to mean "true philosophers". This proverb is of course reminiscent of the Biblical, "For many be called, but few chosen" (Matth. 20:16).

et circenses and the practical issues of everyday as well as professional life and accordingly do not have an "organ" for it. Others may long for it, but their souls (not necessarily their intellect, although that often too) are not subtle enough for it.

Here I am reminded of Goethe's conviction that there are "*Rangordnungen der Seelen*" (ranking orders of souls, or as he in this text sometimes also says instead of "souls", *monads*, using a Leibnizian term that was at times also used by Jung. He uses this phrase about the *Rangordnungen* in a conversation with the scholar and satirical writer Johann Daniel Falk on the day of Christoph Martin Wieland's funeral (January 25, 1813) and in the mood caused by his death.[18] In the course of the discussion, Goethe made a comment that obviously implied that he was convinced that Wieland's soul would, as a matter of course, endure after his death. Asked about it, he explained (after describing the extraordinary format and dignity of Wieland) that "Wieland's soul is by nature a treasure, a true jewel." He categorically declared, "There can never and under no circumstances be any question of the destruction of such high soul forces in nature; it never treats its assets so lavishly." Other souls or monads, by contrast, may not represent the same degree of soul force. For example, occasioned by the noise of a barking dog, Goethe goes as far as to speak derogatorily with respect to such animals of

---

18 Johann Daniel Falk, *Goethe aus näherm Umgang dargestellt* (1832). Here cited from *Goethes Gespräche*. Biedermannsche Ausgabe, augmented and edited by Wolfgang Herwig, vol. 2, München (Deutscher Taschenbuch Verlag) 1998, pp. 769 ff.

4. Psychological Hope

"*Monadenpack*" (something like the rabble of monads). And as far as humans are concerned, souls can be rather light weight, with only little soul substance compared with souls that have the dignity of being "true jewels" by nature.

For us it is noteworthy that Goethe's interest and focus is on "souls" and "monads" and not on "people" or "persons". This means, on the one hand, that he goes, in the spirit of what *we* call the "psychological difference", to "the *other* picture [here, the picture of monads or souls] that looms up" "behind the impressions of the daily life, behind the scenes [here, behind the impression of what is visible, namely people]" (Jung) and that the difference that he makes in the ranking that exists between souls or monads does not refer to external everyday evaluations, not to such distinctions as they exist in social reality, for example, between "the elite" or "celebrities", on the one side, and ordinary people on the other.

On the other hand, it means that "souls", "monads", are for Goethe *realities of nature.* The soul is substantiated in keeping with the metaphysical tradition. This needs to be clearly distinguished from our psychological concept of soul as absolute negativity or spirit. We could say that it is the "soul" in Goethe's nature-based sense that *in people* is receptive or not receptive to the soul's logical life in our psychological sense, as well as the potential *psychic* carrier of it.

I leave aside Goethe's main topic in this conversation,

the thesis of the continuation of souls after the body's death, which in his case, as we have seen is not at all a Christian, not a religious belief,[19] but founded in Goethe's study of nature, nature in his high sense of the word.[20] But with his idea of the "*Rangordnungen der Seelen*" (which is part of his general philosophy of nature and is merely introduced in this spontaneous conversation as an argument to explain and support his view), I think that Goethe has a valid point and that it is a point that *mutatis mutandis* applies also to our topic. "Psychological hope" is only for a few.

This being so, the questions each individual may ask himself is: Have I *really* let myself be reduced by life to *my* "I am *only* that!"? Have I had, and do I have, the courage to face life's fate and the world directly as naked self and *homo totus*—rather than through split-off abstractions of myself glossed over by wishful thinking and neurotic self-deception? Did I, do I really go through life without secret subterfuges, without leading a provisional life, without role playing? Have I really fulfilled the duties that my life situation and my own inner

---

19 Christian belief (and hope) concerning the afterlife is dependent on Christ's resurrection. Cf. "But if there be no resurrection of the dead, then is Christ not risen: ... If Christ has not been raised, your faith is futile and you are still in your sins. ... If our hope in Christ has been for this life only, we are of all people the most pitiable" (1Corinthians 15:13–19). All this plays no role in Goethe's ideas about an afterlife.

20 For a *poetic* presentation and exemplification of Goethe's view concerning the continuation of souls after death one might want to turn to the end of his Faust tragedy (the scenes *Grablegung*, "Burial" and *Bergschluchten*, "Mountain Gorges").

4. Psychological Hope

calling imposed on me? And above all: what *monad* am I?[21]

These questions are presented here as helps for one's self-knowledge and self-assessment, one's becoming able to place oneself. They are not intended as implicit moral demands of how one should, or should have lived. The benefit of the idea of the order of ranks of soul's is also that it frees us from any such pressure. We have to be who we are. No contorted efforts to be more (to be "a higher monad") than we are. Nevertheless,

> Were I standing, Nature, vis-à-vis you one man alone,
> Then it would be worth the trouble to be a human.[22]

---

21 Just as for Kant his three questions, "What can I know?", "What must I do?", and "What may I hope?" come together in the overarching question, "What is man?", so here "what monad am I?" unites and integrates my several questions immediately preceding it.

22 Joh. W. v. Goethe, *Faust. Eine Tragödie*, 5th Act, Mitternacht, lines 11406 f., my translation.
   (*Stünd' ich, Natur, vor dir ein Mann allein,
   Da wär's der Mühe wert, ein Mensch zu sein.*)

Index

absolute negativity 38, 39, 51, 62, 63, 67, 68, 71
adaptation to new world situation
   and historical hangover from the past 32
   difficulty of 31
Aeschylus
   Prometheus Bound 16
afterlife 36, 38, 72
alone with one's self, to be 58
anchor of Man 53, 56, 60
Atlas (mythol. figure) 45, 46
axis mundi 45, 46, 55, 63
"behind the impressions of the daily life" 39, 71
biological hope 15, 18, 43, 57, 66
   and life force 18
   purely psychic 43
Bloch, Ernst 24
boundedness, limitation to the utmost necessary for infinity 65, 66
Buddhism 50
   no longer mythological, but still innocent 41
cardinal virtues 35, 47
causa sui 44, 62
Christian hope 24, 26, 37-39, 42-46, 48-52, 61, 68, 69
   as causa sui 44
   as distilled "world tree" 46, 55
   as equivalent of initiation, on level of reflection 49
   as existential virtue 50
   as distilled, inwardized former world tree 46, 63
   as real presence of the infinite in oneself 53
   as the virtue of hoping against hope 53
   causa sui 44
   expectation of what one does not see yet 35
   hopes for salvation in afterlife 38
   hopes that Christ will come again 36
   is as actuosity 46
   is extendedness from down here to heaven 44, 46
   is "hoping against hope", q.v.
   its intentionality: goes vertically upwards 24, 44
   objectively embodied in a culture or person 45
   represents *existential* aspect 48
   rooted in soul 43
   structural difference from utopian hope 36
   successor to mythol. *axis mundi* 45, 46, 63
   the strength not to give weight to the misery in this world 53
   who hopes in Christian hope? 42
Christianity 25, 27, 35-38, 41, 42, 44, 46, 48, 49, 51, 55, 67, 68
   beyond logical status of mythological stage 40
   has come home to itself after 18 centuries 47
   its novelty: the new logical form of the essential content 47; the Word has become Flesh 48
   metaphysical religion 41
   religion in the status of reflection 41
   rupture this and other world 40
   soul sense vs. people's understanding 37, 38
   uniqueness: negation not "substance" but "subject" 42, 48
   wounded by intrusion of reflection 41
Christ's second coming 50
Cicero 15, 35
coniunctio 46, 48, 51, 55, 56, 63

Index

must be embodied in Man 48
pineal gland as 55
coniunctio oppositorum 48
consciousness
    lagging behind new logic of reality 31
    learning the hard way 32
Contest of Homer and Hesiod 16
contra spem sperare 53
copula
    logic of 41
cosmological scheme/sense 57, 63, 64
    pulled out from under us 56
cosmological space, metaphysical warmth of 57
cosmos, visible world 40, 62
Descartes 55
devil, merely substantiated presence of absolete negativity in Christianity 67
    nothing but logical negation of God 40
distillation 47
Dum spiro spero 15
ethical principles mere pious ego stances 59, 60
evil
    in Christianity: presence of absolute negativity 67
    principle of, see also devil 67
    the "terrible question of evil" 67
    two senses of 20
experiences, introspective 68
    as happenings: *satori* or *unio mystica* 49
    problem of reliance on them instead of knowledge 60, 61
    helpful only as triggers 60
extendedness 46, 63
fairy tales: "one-dimensional" 40
fake metaphysical world in our time 58
Falk, Johann Daniel 70
false prophets 26
fetishization 28, 30

freedom 62
God
    as gone under, sublated into Love 67
    is spirit 47
Goethe, Joh. Wolfgang von 21
    Faust 18, 72, 73
    idea of ranking orders of souls 70, 72
Gothic cathedrals
    as objective embodiment of Christian hope 45
Greeks, archaic
    pessimistic view of life 16, 20, 21
    status of reflection already reached 22
heaven and earth,
    connection/separation of 41, 45, 46, 48, 55, 63
Heavenly Jerusalem 24, 25, 36-38
Hegel 49
Hesiod 16, 17
highest soul value 25, 27, 36, 37
homo totus 64, 65, 68, 72
hope
    "I do not need hope" 9, 23
    and life force 18
    as an evil 17, 18
    as blind 16
    biological 15
    Christian hope, q.v.
    dialectics of 17, 18
    horizontal vs. vertical hoping 36, 37
    ideological hope, q.v.
    in Pandora's box 16-18
    is the negation of its own negation 52
    is totally empty-handed 52
    last thing to die 15
    legitimacy question 13
    phenomenology of 14
    the reality of negativity itself 52
    the strength not to give weight to the misery in this world 53

Index

utopian hope 26, 28, 33, 35, 36, 43
"What may I hope?" 11, 13, 73
"hope against hope" 18, 53
   the real presence of the infinite in oneself 53
hopelessness of the empirical world 53
horizontality 25, 26, 27-31, 36, 37, 57, 58, 62, 63, 65
   horizontal timeline 37
   rules now 56
humanness of human animal 15, 21, 61, 62
   is *causa sui* 62
   is the existence of freedom 62
   not given, merely a vocation 61
   transcendentality 62
"I am only that!" 65, 67, 72
idealistic crimes as logical transgression, deserve harder punishments 33
identity of identity and difference 49
ideological hope 24, 25, 28, 32, 43, 57
   as secularization and corruption of Christian hope 24-26, 35
   belongs to generality of intellect 43
   is brainchild 24
   is ego product 43
   Marxism-Leninism 24
imagination (*Vorstellung*), mode or medium of 38, 46, 55, 62
   is the logical status of mythological stage 40
individual
   "Are you related to something infinite?" 59
   atomic, isolated 57, 65
   counts for something only because of the essential he embodies 45, 59
   must be alone with his self 58
   must be bounded, limited to the utmost 65
infinite, the 45, 50, 52, 59, 60, 62, 64, 65, 68

inner infinity and one's being totally bounded 65
is core of humanness of human animal 62
its real presence in oneself 53
necessity of link with the infinite 44
the new infinite 67
infinity
   has in modernity chance of coming home to itself 62
inflating social goals with metaphysical meaning 27, 28, 31
   illegitimate, but no blame: birth pangs 31
initiation 49
innocence,
innocence, naivety
   loss of 41, 42, 52
   means unwoundedness by reflection 42
   of mythological mind 41
"is not yet, and yet it is already now" 51
Islam 50
   no longer mythological, but not wounded 41
Jacob's ladder 45
Jung, C.G. 20, 25, 32
   about African medicine man loss of role 26
   about Man's twice-born-ness 44
   about necessity of being alone with one's self 58
   about the stars having fallen from heaven 56
   and the "terrible question of evil" 67
   clearly aware of irrevocable loss of religion, metaphysics 25, 26, 29
   his benefit from illness 19, 66
   his mistake: relation to the infinite through inner experience 64
   his mistake "the Self" instead of total "me" 64, 66

Index

on consciousness of confinement being attached to limitlessness 65
on extramundane authority as counterpoise to the "world" 60, 64, 67
on forging an I that does not break down 66, 67
on necessity of link with the infinite 44, 59
sounding at times like false prophet 26
"Yes" to life 20, 66, 67
Kant, Immanuel 12, 13
his three/four questions 11, 12, 73
knowing, concept of
not "knowing about...", but *embodied* knowing 63, 64
La Rochefoucauld, François de 15
limitation, utmost boundedness 58, 65, 66
logic
of mode of being-in-the-world 69
of the copula 41
of reality, life 31
revolutionized 32
loss of metaphysics, verticality, transcendence 25, 56
African medicine man's loss of role 26
as a veritable gift of history 57
condition of possibility of psychology 56, 57
loss of innocence, see innocence
Love, as the former, sublated God 67
Lüthi, Max 40
Man (see also humanness; individual)
as the Word having become Flesh 56
has to give birth to himself 61
his transcendentality 61, 62
is essentially upwards-looking 56
is fundamentally more than the human animal 44, 52
mortality 16

needs link with the infinite 44
twice-born 44, 45, 48
mandala pictures 68
Marxism-Leninism (see also utopian thinking; ideological hope) 24, 26, 27, 33
Meister Eckhart 49
Mephistopheles 18-20
negation of life 19
metaphysical hope 35
exemplified by Christian hope (q.v.) 35, 55
is a standard not to fall short of 59
metaphysics, metaphysical tradition 11-13, 25-28, 30, 31
loss of 25
resurrected as *philosophia perennis* 26
Mnemosyne 12
modernity 25, 26, 32, 58, 62
loss of religion, metaphysics, q.v.
transition to 25, 32
monads 70, 71, 73
rabble of monads 71
mystery rites 69
mysticism 49
mythological mind/stage
naivety, innocence 41
naturalism, naturalistic mind 48, 50, 62
in mythology, vs. thought, reflection 41
negation, pessimistic view of life
as evil 19, 21
as logically higher status 21
Nietzsche, Friedrich
"Remain faithful to the earth!" 28
"Not to be born is best" 16, 17, 19
numen of salvation 27, 28
obsolescence
an "outdated and never recurring world" 25
Odysseus 41
"opium for the people" 37
"the other picture that looms up" 71

Index

Pandora 16, 17
panem et circenses, modern form of 69, 70
participation mystique with nature 49, 52
pineal gland 55
Plato 69
The Republic 35
projection (see also substantiation; cosmological scheme)
   into externality 46, 62
   into temporality 37
   into the vertical dimension of the cosmos 55, 56
Prometheus 16
psychological difference 71
psychological hope 55
   exists as Man's *internal* extendedness from empirical animal to infinity 63
   is hope's having become a knowing 61
   metaphysical hope as minimum standard 59
   must be fully interiorized into itself 60
   is not relation *to* infinity but infinity as Man's own being 60
   only for individuals, not for the generality 69
   only for the few 69, 72
   presupposes relentless commitment to horizontality 58
psychologists
   duty to take standpoint of soul, not of people 39
psychology
   relies on knowledge, not experiences 61
real life, fateful events
   are what forges an unshakeable I 67, 68
reflection
   status of, in early Greek soul 22
   wounded by intrusion of reflection 41
reflection
   Christian hope as equivalent of initiation, on level of reflection 49
   Christianity as religion in status of reflection 41
   Christianity gives birth to stage of reflection and distillation 47
religion 12, 50, 67
   as a pupation 55
   loss of (see also loss of metaphysics) 56
   mode of *Vorstellung*, projection 55, 56
rescue the world, wish to
   as logical violence, and if acted out as evil 33
sacrificial killings 50
semantic vs. syntactic 37, 40, 42, 47
sempiternitas 62
Sophocles
   Oedipus at Colonus 16
soul
   continuation of souls after the body's death 70, 72
   immortality of 11-13
   modernity is where now its truth is 58
   modern sense of 12
   ranking orders of souls 70
   understands even deficient imaginal presentations correctly 38, 39
   vs. consciousness, ego, people 31, 37, 38
speculative sentence 29, 52
Stalin, Joseph 27
substance has become subject 42, 46
substantiation (see also projection) 46, 55, 66-68, 71
superstition 37, 38
syntactic see semantic
temptation of looking backwards to old metaphysical world 58
Teresa of Ávila 49

Index

"the stars have fallen from heaven" 56
"the Word has become Flesh" 48, 50, 52
Theognis 16
thisworldly, thisworldliness 25, 27, 29, 57
transcendence, trancendent 25, 28, 56, 58
   loss of, see loss of metaphysics
unio mystica 49
upwards orientation (see also infinity; transcendence) 24, 35, 44, 45, 50, 56, 63
utopian thinking 25-27, 30, 33
   as secularization of Christian hope 24
   atrocities committed in the name of 33
   is illegitimate 27, 30
   is not "horizontal" enough 26
   took over the *numen* of salvation 27
value
   as market value or as subjective value 29
   "the whole value of life" 30
verticality 25-28, 29, 30, 32, 35-37, 41, 44, 50, 56-58, 63
"we count for something only because of the essential we embody" 45
Wieland, Christoph Martin, "his soul by nature a true jewel" 70
world ash, world tree 45, 55, 46
   inwardized former 63, 68
world, empirical
   its hopelessness 53
Zen Buddhism 42
   no longer mythological, nevertheless not wounded 42
   Zen satori 49
Zeus 16

Other Titles in English by Wolfgang Giegerich

The Soul's Logical Life: Towards a Rigorous Notion of Psychology, Frankfurt am Main, et al. (Peter Lang) 1998, 5th edition 2020.

(with David L. Miller, Greg Mogenson) *Dialectics and Analytical Psychology: The El Capitan Canyon Seminar*, New Orleans (Spring Journal Books) 2005, now: London and New York (Routledge) 2020.

The Neurosis of Psychology. Primary Papers towards a Critical Psychologie. (= W.G., Collected English Papers, vol. 1) New Orleans (Spring Journal Books) 2006, now: London and New York (Routledge) 2020.

Technology and the Soul. From the Nuclear Bomb to the World Wide Web. (= W.G., Collected English Papers, vol. 2) New Orleans (Spring Journal Books) 2007, now: London and New York (Routledge) 2020.

Soul-Violence. (= W.G., Collected English Papers, vol. 3) New Orleans, LA (Spring Journal Books) 2008, now: London and New York (Routledge) 2020.

The Soul Always Thinks. (= W.G., Collected English Papers, vol. 4) New Orleans, LA (Spring Journal Books) 2010, now: London and New York (Routledge) 2020.

What Is Soul? New Orleans, LA (Spring Journal Books) 2012, now: London and New York (Routledge) 2020.

The Flight Into The Unconscious. An Analysis of C.G. Jung's Psychology Project (= W.G., Collected English Papers, vol. 5) New Orleans, LA (Spring Journal Books) 2013, now: London and New York (Routledge) 2020.

Neurosis. The Logic of a Metaphysical Illness, New Orleans, LA (Spring Journal Books) 2013, now: London and New York (Routledge) 2020.

"Dreaming the Myth Onwards": C.G. Jung on Christianity and on Hegel. Part 2 of The Flight Into the Unconscious (= W.G., Collected English Papers, vol. 6) New Orleans, LA (Spring Journal Books) 2013, now: London and New York (Routledge) 2020.

Pitfalls in Comparing Buddhist and Western Psychology: A contribution to psychology's self-clarification, ISPDI Monograph Series, vol. 2, 2018.

The Historical Emergence of the I. Essays about one Chapter of the History of the Soul, London, Ontario (Dusk Owl Books) 2020.

Working With Dreams. Initiation into the Soul's Speaking About Itself, London and New York (Routledge) 2021.

(with Marco Heleno Barreto) *Human Dignity and the Garden of Eden Story. Distinctions, Disputations, and New Insights*. Ed. by Greg Mogenson. With an Introduction by Peter White. London, Ontario (Dusk Owl Books) 2024.

How to Think Psychologically: With Jung Beyond Jung, (= W.G., Collected English Papers, vol. 7), London and New York (Routledge), forthcoming.

Sharpening Psychology's Concepts: The Spirit of Jungian Psychology and the Danger of Faulty Thinking, (= W.G., Collected English Papers, vol. 8), London and New York (Routledge), forthcoming.

www.ingramcontent.com/pod-product-compliance
Lightning Source LLC
Chambersburg PA
CBHW051712040426
42446CB00008B/839